JAMES ARTHUR

Nadia Cohen

Foreword by Alice Hudson

**FLAME TREE
PUBLISHING**

Contents

JAMES ARTHUR

UNOFFICIAL

Publisher and Creative Director: Nick Wells
Project Editor: Polly Prior
Picture Research: Emma Chafer and Polly Prior
Art Director and Layout Design: Mike Spender
Layout Design: Jane Ashley
Digital Design and Production: Chris Herbert

Special thanks to: Laura Bulbeck, Emma Chafer, Esme Chapman and Daniela Nava

FLAME TREE PUBLISHING
Crabtree Hall, Crabtree Lane
Fulham, London SW6 6TY
United Kingdom
www.flametreepublishing.com

Website for this book: www.flametreepop.com

First published 2013

13 15 17 16 14
1 3 5 7 9 10 8 6 4 2

ISBN 978-0-85775-874-3

Printed in China

Foreword

On 9 December 2012, James Arthur became the UK's ninth *X Factor* winner. And so the 24 year old from tiny Saltburn became the latest willing victim launched headfirst into that crazy whirlwind of instant fame. Hunky, tattooed Arthur differs from previous *X Factor* champs. The first winner ever to have toiled in the dreaded 'bottom two' has since enjoyed the best early commercial success in the show's history. 'Impossible', Arthur's debut, was not only the fastest selling UK track of 2012 but by February 2013, had shifted 1.3 million copies, a new *X Factor* record.

But perhaps the biggest difference about gravelly-voiced, guitar-strumming, rapping James Arthur is that unlike previous champions, he was no wannabe popstar, but already a dedicated – albeit struggling – musician when he chose to audition. Wowing at the Newcastle try-outs with his own take on judge Tulisa's track 'Young', James penned his first song aged 15 and gigged in alt/prog rock bands like Moonlight Drive, Cue The Drama and Save Arcade. Members of Middlesbrough's local 'scene' were naturally stunned to see Arthur up there, killing it on the *X Factor* stage. With his piercing blue eyes, long lashes and 6 ft 3 in frame, JA certainly never had to prove his pulling power with the ladies.

Yet as we go to print he remains desperate to prove he's no one-hit-wonder while fighting to the teeth for control of the full-length album his new fans are pining for. James understands – probably more than any previous winner – that longevity just simply isn't guaranteed in the music business, no matter how talented you are.

Best of luck James, it may be early days but remember there are plenty of us backing you all the way!

Alice Hudson

An Impossible Dream

When an angry-looking lad stumbled into the *X Factor* auditions in 2012, he looked as if he would rather be anywhere else in the world. James Arthur's mumbled attempts at conversation at first failed to impress the notoriously tough judging panel – Gary Barlow, Nicole Scherzinger, Tulisa Contostavlos and Louis Walsh – who exchanged worried glances and prepared for yet another wannabe contestant flunking their audition.

However, the moment James started to sing, they knew that they had found a star. Totally lost in the song, he was amazed, when he opened his eyes, to discover that the entire audience and the judges were on their feet, rewarding his performance with a lengthy standing ovation.

'He is real as a person and I connect with him more than any other contestant. He is honest and real with his music too.'

Tulisa on James Arthur

The X Factor

& Simco Ltd.

The X Factor

*'I think you're brilliant. I love everything
about you and if I was at home right now
I would be voting for you.'
Gary Barlow on James Arthur*

Tough Times

After years as a struggling singer-songwriter, failing to reach the level of success he dreamt of while living in a rundown bedsit in Middlesbrough, James had almost given up hope of ever finding fame. He had fought a tough battle with crippling depression and even ended up sleeping on the streets during a particularly tough time in his troubled teen years.

However, his unconventional attitude to the famous TV talent show immediately won James an army of sympathetic fans who voted him through week after week. He quickly emerged as one of the favourite contestants – and one of the hardest to beat – although in the final he was given a run for his money by his rival Jahmene Douglas.

Eventually, though, James proved triumphant and Simon Cowell immediately signed him to his record label Syco on a lucrative deal: James's greatest dream had finally come true.

'I get the guitar out and start singing at the top of my voice until I feel any anxiety draining away.'

James Arthur

'It felt like we both won, it could

have been either one of us.'

James Arthur on fellow X Factor

finalist Jahmene Douglas

Stunning Success

James was stunned by his overnight success. Within hours of its release, his debut single 'Impossible' hit the No. 1 spot in the British charts and became the fastest selling single ever by an *X Factor* winner when a staggering 1.3 million copies had been sold by February 2013.

James never imagined he would make it to the top. In 2011 he had auditioned for BBC1's rival singing show *The Voice* and made it into the final 200 contestants but no further, leaving his already fragile confidence in pieces.

'This time last year I was nowhere.

I've had to sleep rough. It's hard to

forget things like that.'

James Arthur

Early Struggles

The *X Factor* judging panel were deeply moved when they heard how James's life had spiralled out of control when he was just 14, after his mother Shirley and stepfather Ronald Rafferty split up. It meant that he had to give up a charmed life at private school in Bahrain to move back to Britain with his mother.

He found the transition back to the Northeast difficult and he struggled to fit in at school. Rebelling both in and out of the classroom, James's parents and teachers found him increasingly difficult to manage.

His description of that time is heartbreaking: 'I started sleeping rough when I was 15. I got kicked out of my mum's house and I didn't really care where I slept. I understand why she chucked me out because I was unbearable to live with. She couldn't cope with me because I was so angry.'

'I was really worried because I felt ready to give up on life. Who knows how bad it could have got?'

James Arthur

'The thing I've found hardest is going
from being a normal person to feeling as
though I have to expose myself.'

James Arthur on fame

At A Dead End

That period in James's life was tough: his relationship with his mother had deteriorated to the point where the damage done appeared to be beyond repair. 'I didn't have a male role model and I couldn't relate to her so I lashed out at her. I either crashed on someone's couch or a park bench. I was a pretty tough kid, but I had to steal food a couple of times. I went to supermarkets like Sainsbury's and filled up a plastic bag to try to steal enough food for the week. They did catch me once or twice, but they never called the police – just told me not to come back.'

James ended up in foster care for two years but found he longed to be reunited with his biological family. It was not until he proved his maturity at the *X Factor* auditions that he felt he had something to offer. 'My lowest point was when I was living with a family that I didn't know and I would look at pictures of my sisters and I wanted to be around them. It was really hard not being able to see them,' he recalled later.

'My son is not materialistic at all.
What he will love is spending quality
time with me and the girls [his sisters]
more than anything.'
Shirley, James Arthur's mum

'I'm living in five star hotels,
I was in a bedsit before this,
my music was being heard
by a few people before this,
now millions of people
are hearing it.'
James Arthur on his
X Factor success

Working Class Hero

James Andrew Arthur was born on 2 March 1988 and – after his parents Shirley and Neil split up when he was very young – grew up with his mother, a former fashion model, in Redcar. He has two older siblings, Neil and Sian, as well as three younger step-sisters, Charlotte, Jasmine and Neve, and remains close to them all.

For The Love Of Music

Times were tough for Shirley: James suffered from ADHD (attention deficit hyperactivity disorder) and, after crashing into a glass table at the age of five, he was left with a lazy eye because he had severed some of his nerves.

Music was always James's first love: he started singing when he was just six years old and found himself joining in with his mother's favourite Michael Jackson and David Bowie albums. His talent was obvious from the start but his parents could not have predicted what lay ahead for him. Although he adored singing and writing his own songs from an early age, he also shone at English, and writing imaginative stories and poetry, which impressed his teachers.

'Sometimes I can't sleep, I've got that many creative ideas going round my head.'

James Arthur

'The show has produced a lot of talent from the North East, it has nurtured people like Amelia Lily and the girls from Little Mix and Joe McElderry, I would like to carry on flying the flag for the North East.'

James Arthur

From The Good Times…

Seven years after her divorce from Neil, James' mother Shirley remarried, and the family moved to Bahrain where her new husband Ronald worked. It was a happy time for James who recalled how the family lived a far more luxurious life: 'I was at a private school and we lived in a nice villa with pools.'

James remembers the years he spent in Bahrain fondly; it was the first time he performed in public, in school productions of the musicals *Oliver!* and *The Pirates of Penzance*. 'I had a lot more confidence back then, so I just used to dive in without thinking. I was a bit of a loudmouth … and I was pretty laid-back and happy,' he said.

His performances won him a great deal of praise, on which James thrived, but when his mother and stepdad Ronald got divorced, he moved back to his hometown in Britain, where he recalls immediately feeling like an outsider.

'[After] my mum and stepdad split up, we moved back to England to a two-bedroom house and I got a bit lost. The contrast between lifestyles was a shock. Going back to working-class Britain tipped me off the rails at school and I didn't have a lot to believe in. I used to vent my frustration at the teachers.'

'I've got a lot of respect for the man. He's done a lot for the music industry in terms of the fact he's changed people's lives.'

James Arthur on Simon Cowell

…To The Bad

His new local state school was a very different environment to the private school in Bahrain, where James feared he would be bullied for enjoying singing and dancing. He explained, 'I stopped having anything to do with singing and I became the class clown instead!'

James quickly toughened up to fit in with his new classmates but, as a result of his negative attitude, he was constantly in trouble at school: 'I ended up being a truant and missing a lot of school. I've been in trouble with the police and got my wrists slapped a few times on nights out for fighting. But I'd never go out and try to intentionally harm anyone.'

'In my life before this, the best thing I ever did for anyone was probably lend them a quid or something, but it's nice to see the reaction on people's faces and making them happy.'

James Arthur

Moreover, his disruptive behaviour was causing enormous problems at home. James had lost touch with his father and, as his mother soon found that she was unable to cope with her wayward son, he ended up choosing to live in foster care for his last year of school. Although it was his decision to move away from home, he kept it secret from his friends. 'I was unbearable to live with,' he admitted. 'I hated seeing how much my behaviour hurt my mum but I didn't seem to be able to stop myself.'

Emotional Release

Although he was a tearaway, by the age of 16 James had realized that being good at singing had become cool again and that his talent was starting to impress his friends. 'Music was a coping mechanism for me,' he said. 'It was my escape when everything else around me was rubbish.'

Influenced by Nirvana, Eminem and Black Sabbath, James taught himself to play the guitar and started to pour out his troubled emotions into song lyrics, which helped him to deal with all the changes he was going through.

After leaving school with barely a handful of GCSEs, the future looked bleak for James. He went on to study music at college but dropped out of the course after just a year, having failed to turn up to many classes.

'I don't think I need a year away being trained or told how to perform.'

James Arthur

Without A Trace

He formed his first band, called Traceless, with some friends and although they performed locally and James managed to earn enough money to pay the rent on his first flat, he never imagined music could be a career for him. Evicted from his apartment for holding too many wild parties, James soon ended up homeless and his situation became so dire that he had to steal food in order to survive.

He said, 'There were a few times when I found myself with nowhere to live, but I was too embarrassed to tell people, so I ended up sleeping rough. It was something I had to do to survive, so I just got on with it.' Although he would return to his mother's house occasionally, he was a disruptive influence on the family; moreover, he was determined to support himself.

'I'm just achieving goals, left, right and centre and I just feel incredibly lucky because I never thought it would happen. The contrast in lifestyles is huge.'

James Arthur

Getting By

When Traceless split up, he joined another band called Cue The Drama, followed by Heroes and Hand Grenades, and he later formed a group called The Emerald Sky. With his next band, Moonlight Drive, he made several studio recordings through a contact he had made by performing in local venues. It was his first taste of success but Moonlight Drive only found limited fame in the local area.

He then had the opportunity to record a few of his own songs and started performing as The James Arthur Band. Although things were moving in the right direction for James, instead of being excited at the potential, he found himself increasingly frustrated at his lack of progress.

He found several different jobs, one in a call centre and another being hired to write CVs in a local office but James knew these roles were not for him. 'They were all dead-end jobs and just a way to get by really,' he said.

Turning The Tide?

By the time he was 23, James was suffering badly from depression and had decided to try to turn his life around, first of all by apologizing to his parents for his destructive behaviour over the years. 'I was spending a lot of time in bed and feeling low,' he commented. 'Things felt a bit hopeless. I didn't think I was ever going to get anywhere.'

Determined to pull him through this low period in his life, friends urged James to audition for *The X Factor*. He was at first reluctant because he felt he did not fit the image of the show but eventually he borrowed £10 for the train fare to Newcastle and plucked up the courage to sing Tulisa's song 'Young' in front of the judges.

'You know it's funny because I think all the people who say they hate it, watch it, and I think a lot of people who say they hate it are hypocrites because they all comment on it and people always talk about it, so whether you love it or hate it, I bet they're sat in front of the telly on Saturday night watching it.'

James Arthur